W9-BYB-107

For Mel —
A pleasure to meet you
& work with you here
at Sewanee, 2009 —

Andrew Hudgins

BABYLON IN A JAR

NEW POEMS

Andrew Hudgins

A MARINER BOOK
Houghton Mifflin Company
BOSTON NEW YORK

First Mariner Books edition 2001

Copyright © 1998 by Andrew Hudgins
All rights reserved

For information about permission to reproduce selections from
this book, write to Permissions, Houghton Mifflin Company,
215 Park Avenue South, New York, New York 10003.

Visit our Web site: www.houghtonmifflinbooks.com.

Library of Congress Cataloging-in-Publication Data
Hudgins, Andrew.
    Babylon in a jar : new poems / Andrew Hudgins.
      p. cm.
    ISBN 0-395-90994-5
    ISBN 0-618-12697-x (pbk.)
    I. Title.
  PS3558.U288B3 1998
  811'.54—dc21   98-11865 CIP

Book design by Lisa Diercks
Typeset in Monotype Dante

Printed in the United States of America

QUM 10 9 8 7 6 5 4 3 2 1

For Erin

You can look out of any window of time
and catch sight of still another face of God.
Lean out of the time of sedge and warblers:
God caresses.
Lean out of the time of Moses and Elias:
God haggles.
Lean out of the time of the Cross:
God's face is all blood, like Veronica's napkin.
Lean out of your own time:
God is old, bent over a book.

—Sándor Weöres, from "The Colonnade of Teeth,"
    translated by Edwin Morgan

CONTENTS

1

THE CHINABERRY

I couldn't stand still watching them forever,
but when I moved
                    the grackles covering
each branch and twig
                        sprang
                                together into flight
and for a moment in midair they held
the tree's shape,
                    the black tree
                                peeling from the green,
as if
        they were its shadow or its soul, before
they scattered,
                    circled and
                                re-formed
as grackles heading south for winter grain fields.
Oh, it
        was just a chinaberry tree,
the birds were simply grackles.
                                A miracle
made from this world and where I stood in it.
But you can't know how long
                                I stood there watching.
And you can't know how desperate I'd become
advancing
            each step on the feet of my
advancing shadow,
                    how bitter and afraid I was
matching step after step with the underworld,
my ominous, indistinct and mirror image
darkening with
                extreme and antic nothings

the ground I walked on,
                              inexact reversals,
elongated and foreshortened parodies
of each
            foot lowering itself
                              onto its shadow.
And you can't know how I had tried to force
the moment, make it happen
                              before it happened—
not necessarily this
                              though this is what I saw:
black birds deserting the tree they had become,
becoming,
            for a moment in midair,
the chinaberry's shadow for a moment
after they had ceased to be
                              the chinaberry,
then scattering:
                  meaning after meaning—
birds strewn across the morning like flung gravel
until
      they found themselves again as grackles,
found each other,
                  found South
                              and headed there,
while I stood before
                  the green, abandoned tree.

AFTER MUSCLING THROUGH SHARP
  GREENERY

After muscling through sharp greenery and after
lopping humped limbs back
                          as far as lopping shears
would take them
                  and after sawing
the amputated limbs to a single stump
and after
          I'd heaped the branches in a pile
and ground them down to mulch—sweet,
                                      sticky chips—
I soaked the August clay to soften it,
and began to dig. Pick,
                        then shovel. Pick,
then shovel.
              I rocked the loose stump, rowing it
and popping roots, but couldn't
                                drag it free.
I traced the yew roots deep.
I tore and teased them from the greasy clay,
tugged and pulled and chopped
                              until the stump
sagged in the ground, unfixed. And now I own
what I desire:
              a hole,
a nothing I can fill with anything.
But for a long
              time I will leave it empty
before I make it something and diminish it
with paper-whites,
                    the redbud's gnarled
                                          calligraphy,
azaleas red as every word that Jesus uttered.

POEM

Blunt daffodil spikes
—Babylon and Nineveh—
split frozen earth. They're yellow,
the coarse dead yellow
they died back to
last summer, leaf tips
returning as pale flames:
unburied candelabra, a dead
queen rising from below,
led by a cold torch.
Sparta, Athens, Rome.
Mecca and Medina. From underneath,
blades bayonet the ice-crazed
black crust, the blade tips
yellow, tinged with last
year's death and, already erect
—Beijing, Paris, Rome—
they green, they come alive.
Moscow, Berlin, Tokyo.
The murderous, back-
from-death preblossoming
blossoms, promising
the frilled afterthought
of flowers, bright cups
tipping in the March god's fist.
Jerusalem. Tyre and Sidon.
They are not cups. But watch
bees drink from their crimped lips.
Tenochtitlán and Sumer.
Frail blade, but see what it
destroys. Cold fire, but feel
the dead world's constant simmer.

ASHES

My left hand joggled Johnny's arm, and Johnny
—Jesus!—
                Johnny dropped the coffee can
holding his sister. The can
                                rolled jerkily,
the lid
        spun off, and Sister Rachel spilled
across the black linoleum.
Did I mention we'd been drinking? Everyone
stepped back,
                then back again.
                                Who wants
to track a woman's ashes on the floor
of a rented hall, then get home
                                slightly drunk,
pull off his dress shoes and find a residue
of fine dust
            trapped in the polished leather creases,
especially if it's dust
                        you know by name
and flirted with
                ungracefully a time or two:
"Nice shoes. I love those
                        strap sandals." Rachel Fuller.

A few
    drunk mourners gasped, a few
                                more giggled,
and since I was the one who knocked her loose
I rooted in the kitchen,
                        found a broom,

but Johnny
          wrestled the splayed broom from my hands
and slapped the heavy ash and particles
of crushed bone toward the can.
                              "Come on now, Rachel,"
he said, "you
              wild woman you," and weeping,
Johnny stabbed and swatted at the floor
until I found a paper towel,
                         wet it,
and mopped
          the last fine dust.
                              But what next?
At home I left it on the dresser. A month.
Three months.
              "Throw that revolting thing away!"
my wife said.
              Six months.
                         "Why are you keeping it?"
Rachel Fuller. Old possibility.
A little loud.
              Sharp. Quick.
                         A little sexy.
But what do I know? I met her at a party,
admired her taut,
                 tan calves,
                              but praised her shoes,
and thought
          she might have been a little sorry
I couldn't find the sly
                       next words to say.
Eight months her ashes challenged me to grieve.
But I kept waiting
                  and, as I knew it would,

the magic
        leached away, the awe
                withdrew,
and I disposed of it, her dust, as we do
almost all
        the dead—even those
                we loved,
loved utterly—
        because they are sheer dust
and should be honored as the dust they are.

IN THE RED SEATS

High in the red seats'
vertiginous, steep,
narrow rows, I stood
to let four drunks edge by,
and one, back turned to the field,
side-shuffled down the row,
shouting, "Hi! Great game!"
into averted faces.
Great game? It was nothing-
nothing in the first inning.
He breathed beer in my face. Our eyes
met and the force of meeting
seemed to tip him backward. He teetered,
flailed. I reached out, grabbed
his shoulder, pulled him erect
and past erect till we
were leaning forehead to forehead,
touching, and his eyes
flooded with love. He tossed
both arms around me, sobbed,
"You saved my life, man.
I swear I'll never forget you."
"Yeah, sure you will," I said
and slapped his back,
a quick, bluff way of saying,
"You're okay, pal" and "Hey,
let go." He nodded, shuffled
to his seat with his drunk buddies,
and one, as he slid past,
bobbed his eyebrows at me
and shrugged.
                Five seats away,

from an adoring, pink,
intoxicated face,
love shimmered, love radiated
like equatorial sunshine,
the way a lover's face
illuminates the lover,
the loved, and the dark world
in one strange, lucent moment:
satisfied and thrilled, intense
and effortless—as God
regards us every moment.
I couldn't bear it. I left
in the fifth inning, sidling
down packed precipitous
red rows, easing past strangers,
excusing myself.

EDGE

Nicked steel wears down the waterstone
and the waterstone

                 grinds dull nicked steel
till it reveals a bright

                   undamaged edge.
I hone it on a fine black Arkansas,
strop it

          ten times on jeweler's rouge, then

                          eye
the polished steel, turning it back and forth,
and catch

         my smudged, unshaven face
in mirrored steel, almost satisfied,
a man who,

           though he knows it's backward, loves,
sometimes, the sharp

                edge more than anything
he's made with it

             because it's easy
to slip,

        gouge tiger maple, miscut cherry,
and soon exotic scrap rises

                waist high
beside the cast-iron stove, while I stand scraping

                         bright
unblemished steel against the waterstone,
warmed by the fire of my

              expensive failures.

DRAGONFLY

Book says "most predacious." Book
says "fastest
        flying insect," says
it eats its body weight in half an hour.
Mother called it
        the devil's
darning needle. Book
             adds "darner"
and "devil's arrow." Mother said
it stitches shut the eyes,
            ears, lips
of sleeping children, and Book confirms
that mothers would say that.
              Book says
dragonflies can
        snap a gnat
in mid-
        air, eat it on the wing,
and Book says what I've always called
a dragonfly is really,
           with its
long
    slender body, a
           damselfly
that strafes the pond clabber, soars,
swoops,
        hovers, sideslips, loops
             and twists,
sunlight revealing a new glint
of iridescent
        shimmer—purple, red,
green, turquoise, gold, gunmetal blue—

with every pass.
                    It's hunting: a whip
tip
    cracking gnats
                    out of the air
so quick that I can't see it happen
and wouldn't know except I trust
Book, Book,
                    the goddamn book because
I cannot see the hunting. See
what looks like
                    exhilaration
                            (loop
                                    and soar),
but isn't. Book insists on purpose.
Not even blood sport. Work.
                            But its purpose
is not
        my purpose: pleasure
                            (dive, jink, roll,
then
        stillness at great speed)
                            beside still water.

NIGHT CLASS

He'd pull a yellow clipping from his wallet,
and while you read it he stared in your face.
The other students scanned the clipping, nodded,
smiled as best they could, and gave it back
to the pudgy, sweaty boy, who grinned at them
expectantly.
               They complained, and finally
I stopped him after class.
                         "Uh, Mister Kearny,
maybe you shouldn't, uh, share with your friends
about shooting your father."
                         "I didn't shoot him."
"You didn't?"
                    "No sir, I hit him with a bat.
See, he was whipping on my mom again
and whipping on me too and then one day
I just got tired of being whipped on
and I hit him with my uncle's metal bat
and just kept hitting till he didn't move.
I didn't mean to kill him, just make him stop."
His high voice trembled, his eyes were fixed on mine.
"I got my picture in the paper." He reached
back toward his hip. "You want to see the clipping?"

"That clipping, Mister Kearny, that's the problem.
People get very nervous around somebody
who's killed somebody—no matter why he killed them.
Now maybe that's unfair, but if you think
about it, I'm sure you'll understand it's true."

He stared down the emptying hall
at a few students heading to their cars,

their late jobs, home.

> "Does that make sense to you?"

The twin fire doors wheezed shut behind two girls.
His face deepened to a face I've come
to think of, on other faces, as ancient, accepting.

"That makes sense to you, now doesn't it?"
I said, a little sharply.

> "Yeah, I guess."

He was whispering.

> "Good, Peter. I'm glad.

Now don't forget the paper that's due Friday."

He pushed his way into the stairwell. I waited
until I heard the outside door clank shut
before I followed. I wanted to be the one
whose leaving let the hall fall into silence —
silence which I have, from talking, learned to love.
But what, when no one loved me, have I done
but talk, talk, talk until I've said, like Peter,
the thing I shouldn't say or, like tonight,
until I've said exactly what I had to say.
And as I hurtled home past dark, tires wailing,
I howled with every song on the radio,
screamed some teenage stranger's stupid words,
shrieked somebody else's rage, somebody's love,
till I could bear my own voice, and its silence.

ONE THREW A DIRT CLOD AND IT RAN

One threw a dirt clod and it ran, and when it paused,
another threw a rock and it trotted out of range,
so they pursued it, lobbing rocks and sticks,
just to see it gallop, which was beautiful,
then to keep it running, but when it stumbled on barbed wire
and broke a front leg and crumpled to its knees, entangled,
one hit it with a tree limb and hit it again. It fell
and they, laughing, ran up and kicked it, jumped away,
ran off, ran back and kicked it, till they could stand beside it,
kicking. They cheered when one of them pried loose
a broken fence post. They fought for the fence post
and took turns swinging it until the tangled beast's
slack ribs stopped pumping, heaving. Gasping for breath,
they stared at one another, dropped the post, the stones, the sticks.
They nudged the huge corpse and waited for it to rise,
to rise and gallop over rutted, fenced-off fields
as if there were no ruts, no mudholes, scrub brush, wire,
so they could follow it forever, weeping and hurling stones.

SIGNS OF A CHANGE IN WEATHER

The jackdaw chatters late, the chaffinch pipes at dawn,
and in a week the market sets record highs
and record lows. The brown moth turns to gray.
The five-year plan enters its thirteenth year.
Visions grow more frequent among believers,
and bees swirl near the hive, guarding their stores
against an unseen foe, while vodka prices
inch downward and the cost of razor wire skyrockets.
Attacks on Jews and Jewish-owned businesses
increase in frequency and violence. A sudden
massing of elite troops on the border,
and the president preempts Saturday programming
and tells bored children his recurring dream,
bored because they too have dreamed repeatedly
of the steep roof, the book with unturnable pages.
And honeysuckle reeks of burning rubber.

WIND

Wind shook the dead but not-yet-fallen leaves.
Wind tugged and plucked and rattled the dead leaves,
the wind entreating *come* and the oak leaves,
already dead, saying *no* to death, *no*,
for that was what the wind through brown leaves was—death—
and I was afraid: maple leaves called *take me*
and the wind took them, and I was fascinated
because it snatched and pulled at me and I said *no*.
I said *no* but I loved its hands on me,
loved its familiar and insistent touch—
the mild inquiring tug at my shirtsleeve,
the sweeping breeze that stood my limp hair straight,
the wind that slapped my red cheeks, stung my eyes,
puffed my pant legs and ballooned my shirt.
I loved the hard wind, loved it, loved the huge
steps I strode when the wind's muscular hand
clamped on my back and thrust me before it,
its will almost my will, and in its hands
I hated stepping heavier than air,
hated resisting the long wind, which I feared,
so I walked at night to the older parts of town,
where huge oaks hung over houses, soared
across the street and knit together above me,
and I stood in unlit streets on strangers' lawns
so their dark oaks would loom above me also,
moving as hugely as anything I knew
—the sky, the rain, the ocean—with me beneath them
or inside them—which, I wasn't sure;
and the leaves, which longed to be immovable,
flailed, fought—and one by one, fighting, let go
to the wind, the irresistible smooth wind,
and my life, which I had not yet lived,

clung to those oaks and hickories—my life,
my parents', brothers', everybody's lives—
clung to green twigs while the wind was claiming us,
though only I, I thought, only I saw it,
and I kept silent. Perhaps it was a secret.
The vacant limbs, and they were as yet full,
would soon, I understood this, soon leaf out again.
Soon the wind would lift furled yellow leaves,
unfurl them green, and smooth them. Soon the wind
would flood the air with golden dust, warm perfume,
intoxicants of spring that tempt us, tempt us
to run up green hills, roll down them, and forget
the near-percussive thrum, the deep vibration,
half rattle, of brown leaves on brown leaves, the rich
enveloping sound shimmer that haunts the soul
their hymn has summoned, conjured, then cast out,
and they were it, they were my soul because
for the wind we're all the same: already gone,
already gone though we refuse to go—
and the long wind sweeping us away, I longed
to be the wind, which is the deep, untroubled
inhaling or exhaling of our god.
But I was not the wind, or the leaves wholly,
riding without knowing what it was,
the in-breath or out-breath of the Lord,
and as I stood beneath them, listening,
the leaves sang, dying, *Don't die*, and I've obeyed them.

SUPPER

We shared our supper with the flames,
or the shadow of the flames—each candle
in the light of the other casting shadows
across the table, dark flickers of a brilliant flicker,
and the grain of rubbed pine swirled with light
and shadow, shoaled and deepened in the soft
inconstancy of candlelight.
                              With every gesture
the bright flames flinched and then corrected.
Your shrug, my laugh,
                              my nod, your tilting head
—conveyed on air—invited their response.
They bowed their heads, then snapped upright—
a ripple in the gases' fluted yellow silk,
blue silk, transparent silk. I yearned
to touch the rich untouchable fabric, and finger
the sheen beneath its scorching,
but when I reached, it leaned away
decorously, and I did not pursue it, knowing.

But the dark flames reached out, licked the meat,
licked the plate, the fork, and the knife edge.
They licked our faces and our lips—a dry unfelt tongue,
the shadow of the flame consuming nothing,
but stroking everything as if it could
grasp, hold, take, devour. How ardently it hungers
because it cannot have us.
How chaste the bright flame, because it can.

THE DAFFODILS ERUPT IN CLUMPS

The daffodils erupt in clumps
so thick they
                lift a block of dirt
above their heads, raising
                        dark soil
in exaltation, offering
wet earth
                to wet March air. The tight
leaves split and sag. The flowerhead
bulls up-
                ward, tilts the lifted earth.
Hard, cold rain
                        bangs the remnant back,
back through tall stalks, earth
                                to earth,
where it
                belongs, and flowerheads
unfurl their yellow fripperies,
which to us
                are mere loveliness,
though they have work to do, and do it:
honeybee and bumblebee and even moth
ransack and rummage them.
                                But beauty
unfurled for one eye catches many,
and I
        snip flowers for the table,
where, sipping wine like Nero,
                                pensive,
I'll study them as Nero studied
the corpse of Agrippina,
                        handling

the suddenly compliant limbs,
admiring
      one arm, faulting
            one.
"I hadn't known," he said,
         "I hadn't known
my mother was so beautiful."

WE WERE SIMPLY TALKING

We were simply talking, probably work, or relatives
or even Christmas presents, when the car slid
and I corrected, fishtailed and I corrected, then we were gone,
sliding sideways, sliding backward on black ice
and staring into the grill of a diesel tractor, also sliding,
and in that instant I was ready to die.
I saw my wife and was overjoyed that I had married her,
though our marriage was already falling apart,
and I loved the car, a brown Toyota, loved
being warm in the car while it was white, cold, bitter
out in the world we'd lost control of. I loved
every molecule of breath I wasn't taking,
and for the moment I forgave myself every sin
and failure of my life, including this
ridiculous and undignified early death.
The car snapped backward into a frozen ditch.
I sat speechless, shaking, my wife speechless also,
and a man pulled up, a salesman: You folks okay?
Suddenly the radio roared, and by the car
a dog barked wildly and, yes, we were fine.
Fine. We were fine. But what was "fine," I wondered,
and why do we always, always have to speak?

HEAVEN

Between my back fence and the drainage ditch,
the county's
         no man's land, I'd been chopping brush
and forking out
         thick roots—some extra room
for bush beans and potatoes. Had been.
                       I'd stopped.
Before me,
      coiled in weeds,
             a copperhead
jabbed at
      my boots, but I could barely feel it.
Tap tap. I didn't move. A copperhead,
and I could barely feel it!
           I'd armored myself
in long pants, work
        gloves, rubber boots
against
     this weaponed patch of wilderness:
thorns, yellow jackets, nettles, poison oak,
and wild
      blackberry cane—the
            serpent's Eden,
the copperhead's paradise,
          which I had cleared,
hoed into furrows, planted. The brown
           head struck,
bit,
   fought my rubber boots till I could feel,
with joy,
     how much he hated me,

and with the hoe, I hooked
                         the angry snake
and flicked it,
             writhing, across the ditch
into my neighbor's untouched bramble, where
the gray squirrels, rabbits, mice
                         had also fled
from my blade, my
             advancing paradise.

ELEGY FOR THE BEES

At dusk I crouch in greenery and watch the roses
go unplundered, the violets unravished. The chaste
white lily grows more virtuous than ever,
and everywhere I walk, the peonies,
perfumed lasciviously, soften past lush to blowsy, seducing
the bee that isn't there to be seduced
—a sad, unnatural absence in the garden—
the yellow dust untroubled on the stamen,
the pollen ungathered, the seed unmade,
the fruit unformed and therefore never swollen,
not green, not ripe, not plucked and eaten.

Oh, I could stoop over lilies, dabbing
stamen to stigma, anther to pistil, and I do—
a human bumbler in the void,
the swaying limbs and bobbing flowerheads
abuzz with nothing, no ardent bodies
squirming and rooting in the bloom,
ransacking nectar, draped with pollen
like yellow pantaloons, like golden saddlebags.

Each blossom's Rome no longer, for what is Rome
when she has thrown the city gates wide open
and no one enters, and Babylon when she
has pulled down all her seven walls and no one takes her?
And Nineveh, what is she, and what is Egypt
when no one comes to loot the golden dust
with which each empire turns into the next?

BODIES OF WATER

My shoulder twinges where
his twinges and my left ankle
throbs exactly where
his ankle throbs
and pulses. I look down
and my diagonal
handwriting—angular
and tall—mimics his quick
impossible scrawl slanting
from his hand, his short fingers
clenched on the pen,
and the dry skin of my
right hand is blotched, like his,
with early liver spots.
I'm simply enormous with him,
my whole body full
of him: pink face, bald head,
gray stubble—the same as mine,
the same as his. Small ears
and freckled arms the same—
although my lips are fuller,
my build a little slimmer,
I remind myself. Eyes brown,
not blue. My mother's eyes.
But it's him I'm heavy with,
heavy with my father, heavy
with departure. He's becoming me
so he can leave, and when
I walk near bodies of water
they call to us because
we too are bodies of water.
Ocean and lakes pull,

tug, pluck at us, and from
inside me my watery father
leans toward them, pulls, trying
to break free, pulls fiercely
when I walk by the river:
Ohio, Alabama—
it makes no difference; the surge
of huge brown sluggish current
sings, and I hear it singing—
sings to the water shut
in my cells, calling it
to break free—plasma, spittle,
blood and the various
locked pockets of flux. *Break free,*
it croons and carols, chants
and chortles. *Break free, break free*
—the river's song, death's aria—
and from my cells, my father
sings back inside the choir
of voices he's become,
sings with heartbreaking joy
of his desire, his longing,
his need, need, need
to join the river, yes,
he yearns to be the river,
and like the river (*as*
the river, *is* the river)
he aches for the gulf, the sea,
the ocean—all the time-honored
and time-dishonored metaphors
for birth, death and rebirth.
I understand that. But this,
this isn't metaphor.
Or not just metaphor:
it is my father's body
inside me singing with joy

to the river's joys, which
are surge, ebb, eddy, flood
and obliteration. On these
flat pages I too sing,
sing so you will not hear
the sorrow and misunderstanding
I can't hide when I'm talking.
Singing? Is this singing?
I'm trying to sing one song,
not two, one song that's both
my father's song and mine,
writing with (whose is it?)
my familiar, unfamiliar hand.

BABYLON IN A JAR

Driving home past the beer joints on Airport Boulevard,
I counted, on Sunday mornings, the drunks passed out
beside their cars, their bodies pressed slightly into the gravel
and crushed oystershell. I'd never done that, slept the night,
drunk, beside my car, so I envied and hated the drunks slumped in
    the crushed oystershell
because my life was already so ordered and driven by work
that all leisure, from rough drunk to country club swell,
looked romantic to me, romantic because it was impossible.
At work I sold tickets to rich people leaving town,
then stood at the black glass and watched the after-midnight flights
turn into lights, then watched those lights accelerate, rise and dwindle
into darkness and the east—Atlanta and the world. Though I'd've
    denied it,
I wanted to turn into a light myself
so I could rise and disappear. I didn't want
to go anywhere, I simply wanted to be left alone—
and since I knew that was impossible,
I worked and went to school and worked some more,
waiting to see what would happen, and there those drunks were,
nestled into the ground, half buried and asleep, while I sped by,
sleepy myself but sober, very sober. I've never talked
so elegiacally about myself and I don't care for it,
the puzzled arrogance and bland
forgiveness of it, as if I were beyond the night wind's buffeting
and the day wind's bite, as if from my great height of understanding
I'd fade into death, afflicted
with no greater suffering than I can bear.
But it feels so much like wisdom to talk this way.

I finished school, and because I was now married
I kept two jobs and sometimes, briefly, three. Late Sunday afternoons

my wife and I sat on the porch, talking, watching bright water
arc into the air above our yards and our neighbors',
then fall as measured, artificial rain. Children shouted.
Gunshots and laughter wafted from the nearby houses:
the television world—always too much violence,
too much laughter. The lovely fragrance of roasting meat
rose from a dozen grills, including ours, and while we talked
ice cubes clicked in gin, and every now and then
one cracked, a solitary explosion in our hands,
a sound that startled us and sometimes made us laugh.
They weren't what I was living for, those moments.
Perhaps they should have been. But how can I now regret
the accusations and sudden acquiescences, the paltry squabbles
and quick capitulations of young lovers striving
to be dignified, to be *noble,* inside their bitter striving.
How glibly elliptical
these abstractions are! Mumbling, winking—but gracefully! I no
    longer
have much to say about that time, or much to hint. I'm merely
    using these words
for the Olympian pleasure of pronouncing on myself,
and to build a walkway to my new life.
But what life is new? It's the same good life, still mine,
but with—there are only a few ways to say this—a better wife,
better gin, better meat on an equivalent grill outside a better house
in a larger city, with children that for all I know or care
could be the same ones shouting over the hedge, the same
dogs barking in the distance. Not a different life.
A better life. Only shorter.
                              What great height have I attained
that the young me and the person I am now can slip so easily,
like prey, into the crosshairs of my sorrow and pity?
A sip of red wine, the scent of red meat on the grill
and the whole disordered world falls into order.

Driving to work or back from it, I still think of those distant drunks,
not with the rage I felt when I actually saw them,
but gently, as if sentimentality were my reward
for living my life well. I want to lie down with them
on pea gravel and crushed oystershell still warm with the day's heat
and burrow into it and sleep for a long time
and dream someone else's dreams—not live their lives,
just dream their dreams—and wake to whatever you wake to
after such different sleep. Then I'd drive home
and face the consequences. What? I don't know. I can't imagine.
But dreams and memory have consequences,
and when I think of those sleeping drunks, that distant city,
I remember how Sennacherib quieted the heart of Ashur, his bitter
    Assyrian god:
he obliterated Babylon. He burned it—Babylon, that great city—
    razed the charred buildings,
slaughtered the few remaining people, young and old,
but before he flooded the rubble, he swept up the dust of Babylon
to give as presents, and he stored it in a jar.

2

CATCHING BREATH

In: pink and salmon
                maples bright with dying
glow red and yellow against the dark
                        bronze oaks
they're wildly flying into. Out:
                the eyes
give
    back little. Sometimes
                a sentimental tear,
but not for this rich autumnal dying. In:
the scent
      of dying leaves perfumed with burning
before they're even touched with flame. Out:
                      breath.
In: the flush of warm
              flesh growing warmer
beneath my fingertips. Out:
              breath—warmed breath
filling the warmed hollow of an arching throat.
In: breath. Out: spent breath against cold palms,
                    warming.
Above a hot brow,
          cooling it. Across
a lover's neck, inflaming her.
            Spent breath
hangs white in cold air so we may see before us,
however briefly, the lungs
           we're always filling
with our breath, hot or cold—and those lungs breathe
the world's breath back into us.
         In:
            out. Out:
               in.

PLUNGE

I lumbered from the river and worked my way up the slippery bank,
snugging my feet on the foothold roots, which bulged
like scabbed wet knuckles from the slick clay, then I ginger-hopped
across the sharp hot gravel of the track bed
and marched again the precise intervals of the railroad ties
out to the middle of the trestle, where I paused, gathering myself
   into the moment,
not from fear as I had the first time, and the second, but so I could
   live
what I was about to do: jump.
And while the others splashed, swam, explored the moss-enveloped
   banks,
I jumped and climbed and jumped and jumped and jumped
into the red river, jumped into the red river, though it was orange
really, but I will call it red because everyone did,
and because we called it red, red is what I saw,
red as the blood of the lamb (though I had never seen
lamb's blood, only my own blood and my brothers')—
for, to those of us who have been baptized to our full length,
every plunge echoes that plunge into water that is more than water,
and renders every moment after either sacred or blasphemous,
depending on a judgment not my own. I sprang upward, airward, out,
leaping from the rust-red trestle for the second or two of plummet.
Not flight. Plummet. I leapt for the plummet and the splash,
   always the splash, into the hot red river,
and for the noiseless after-plummet plunge through the slow-motion,
mud-blinded airlessness beneath the breathing world
to the river's plush fundament, which also opened to receive me,
   mud billowing,
and though I could not see it, I felt the black mud billow up
around my ankles, knees, and waist—I imagined it—and my legs
swirled into the unseen cloud—soft, satin, feathery, lascivious,

and I feared I'd enter it as fully as I had the river,
where no one could see or hear me. I couldn't even see myself—
    both obliterated,
and the dazzled center of my obviated senses, a fetus in a dream,
    the only
receiver of my sendings: dream, insanity, solipsism—something
    you wake from,
and breaking from underneath the surface I had shattered from above,
I blinked and blinked, as if I were waking and on the verge of
    understanding
what I was waking to, what I was waking to besides sunlight,
hot wind, the eyes of other people, breath, language,
and I lumbered, dripping, to the bank and fumbled for the root knobs,
my uncontrollable eyes turned to the red trestle, where on the spot I
    had leapt from
my footprints waited for my wet feet to obliterate and renew them.

HOW TO STOP

Through the cracked door I saw
                     the jeweler's fine,
white,
     rapid fingers
              flit above my watch.
His head dipped once or twice and then the woman
—his wife, his sister, or the hired help:
                     who knows?—
brought back my watchband, one
                link shorter,
                    fixed.
"Thanks. What do I owe you?"
                 The woman glanced
back toward the dead man, who didn't raise his head
or turn around.
        "Forget it," he called.
                   "Hey, thanks!
Hey, thanks a lot," I said. Two or three bucks
was breakfast, lunch,
          and supper to me then.

Last week I named him from the radio,
and in the paper I first saw his face,
long
   and sad,
        as if he knew some thug
would kill him for a wedding ring.
"But why'd you have to shoot him?" the cops asked.
"I don't know, man.
         I just did. Okay?"

"Forget it," Tommy Posey told me—advice
from a man who had done me a kindness. Brightened
my day, as Hallmark says.

But now that I have begun to talk about him,
how do I
          stop? I could mention
                         my watchband
was now, in fact, too tight, and pinched red welts
into my wrist. Or I could tell you
                         the killer
said, "Look, I want to put all this behind me
and get on with my life." Or
                         I could muse
on Tommy Posey as a link removed,
leaving shadowy
          what he had linked
                         to what—
because I cannot penetrate the shadows.
Or I could
          point out I'm paying off a debt,
or trying to. I could
          shrug my shoulders,
the way I do, when
                         after a drink or two
I tell this story to appall a friend.
I could go on
          forever, trying to stop.
There is no reason for stopping.
                         You just stop.
But leave that good name hanging in the air:
Tommy Posey,
          who'd done me a kindness when I needed one.

ASHES

Bill gripped the can in both hands and dashed it upward,
casting into the March air his cousin, a man
I'd met a time or two, but now a cloud
of ash and bone grit launched above the river,
and the wind, which bloweth where it listeth, this time
amused itself to swirl the ashes overhead
and, at the moment I yawned, it slapped them back
across the clustered mourners. I sucked down
a grainy mouthful of fresh death, coughed, gagged,
and everyone surged toward me, hands outstretched.
They swatted at my dusty hair, brushed death's
gray epaulets off my shoulders and thumped my back
furiously, as if this dust were different
from other dust, and it was—or why would I
have dressed in coat and tie, and stood, head bowed,
on the soft bank of the Black Warrior, watching
huge barge trains humped with coal chug to the Gulf
while some young Baptist mumbled pieties?
I hacked death from my lungs and spat death out
and hacked up more. The mourners drummed the loose
death out of me. "I'm okay. Thanks," I said,
but they kept drumming, drumming on my back.
"Leave me alone!" I snapped, and we all glanced,
ashamed, into each other's ash-dappled faces.
We turned back to the river and its commerce,
the sermon and its commerce, the wind's new commerce,
and breathed it in and breathed it out and breathed it in.

IN ALESIA

In Alesia, our last town, our final stronghold,
we sent our women and our children out.
When Caesar sent them back, we, to feed our warriors,
we let them starve outside the walls of Alesia.
Our men fought well but not as well as Caesar's,
and in Alesia our handsome king conferred on us a choice:
You may kill me or deliver me to Caesar.
We could not kill him. Outside the breached walls of Alesia,
our broken stronghold, we delivered him to Caesar,
and we watched him throw himself down before Caesar
and we watched him throw out his arms, surrendering,
and we heard Caesar speak coldly to him, our handsome king,
and we saw him bound in chains. With scornful clemency
Caesar dismissed us. For a long time we heard nothing.
We plowed our charred fields, using each other as oxen.
Some of us found new gods, and some of those gods were Roman.
We paid our grain levies and, when he demanded them,
we sent our sons to Caesar and he made them soldiers.
In Alesia, we fathered new children and smiled sadly,
remembering our first children, first wives, our handsome king,
and then, in Alesia, we heard they'd kept him caged six years,
six years in a cage, our handsome king, our famous warrior,
six years before they dragged him through their capital,
some gray barbarian from some forgotten war, our handsome king,
our well-nigh savior, a relic of an old war six years settled.
We heard they tortured him and beheaded him, his head
jabbed on a pike and left till it fell off—
as we have ourselves, from time to time, honored the Romans.
We wish now we had killed him, our handsome king—
embraced him, kissed him, killed him, and buried him in Alesia.
If we were Romans, yes, we could have killed him,
and if he were Roman, he'd never have made us choose.

RAIN

It's raining women here in Cincinnati.
Parts of women, parts of one woman?
The police aren't really sure. Last week
they found an arm, a leg, another arm,
and at eleven last night, while I sipped
the meticulously measured
good bourbon of my middle age,
reporters blandly announced the torso,
no horror in their voices—a slight
professional hush to show they're human too
and they're affected by what they tell us.
Not too much, of course. Teevee is not
the place for outrage, those coiffed homunculi
appropriate for weather, sports—nothing
more tragic than lost football games. Let us
save outrage for our private lives.
(Though isn't this my private life?)
Let the family that has not, as yet, missed her
live outraged. For me, it's pity and terror,
then off to bed unpurged of them,
to seek catharsis in my nightmares. There
the search continues. How can we bury her,
the human jigsaw scattered, half lost, half found?

Like the student who rushed up after class,
I thought we'd passed beyond the ancient myths.
"That stuff you said? About the olden times,
blood sacrifice and fate?
That was true then. It's not true anymore,
is it?" She was almost sobbing.
                              Listen,
my undivided sum, unsundered darling,

listen: Attis, Adonis, Christ, Osiris,
the flute player, the cropped green ear of corn,
whom butchery has transformed into gods;
and this poor slaughtered housewife, whore, hitchhiker,
whom we cannot make whole, though we must try.
Fate. Blood obligation. They're in the news.
We live them every day.

But I said, "No,
it's not true anymore. We aren't all Isis.
We won't all be Osiris."
She smiled. I smiled. She wiped her tears.
Let living teach her what it has to teach her.
She's young. American. Let her resist.
But let the red dismembered gods safeguard
her unsevered flesh. Let those whose work it is
die for her and be scattered on the planet:
God's Scavenger Hunt, God's Hide-and-Seek, God's Tag,
You're It. Amputate, then sew. Explode,
then gather. Smash, repair.
Like a small boy with a radio or frog,
we hack and reassemble our old unmurderable gods
so we won't tear each other into pieces.

Eternity's a ball, history is a stick.

PURPLE

As a boy I'd lie in bed and try
                        to rise
up past
            the ceiling light, out through
white gypsum board, plywood and, finally,
through asphalt shingles
                        into warm
night breezes that
                    would waft me,
                                    lighter than air,
where they inclined, for the wind
bloweth
            where it listeth. I don't.
I've more than failed. I've never budged.
My flights
            are merely metaphor:
the purple throat of a shasta lily,
which does not sing and cannot swallow;
the blue
        illusion at the heart
of ice, which does not
                        pulse with blood:
so free of meaning
                    —lily, ice—
I cannot let them be just blue
or purple. I make them
                        royalty
or sorrow. Even the ripe fruit
of my front-
            yard mulberry: I cannot
                            cannot let it be.

Each berry's
                 bursting with a bead
of . . .
          of life, light, newness, meaning
and yet more meaning,
                       like alchemy
which groans
                 to make base into gold
or gold to platinum, or platinum
to something better—
                       by magic
to make the bad world good, the cruel
world kind.

          Beneath the mulberry
and beneath
               the overripe and rotted
fruit that's fallen from it,
                        I plant
new bulbs, and when I'm done, I'm purple—
a purple
          that means nothing, nothing,
my feet, knees, forearms,
                          elbows, hands
stained
          purple with crushed fruit
so I can, all winter long, revel in
next spring, where
                    in the purple shadows
of the mulberry
                   bees clamber the first
grape hyacinth, and the second
                              grape hyacinth
prepares
          its tiny bells for them,

and the third sends up its flower stalk,
and the fourth,

          having rotted over winter,
is now half

        black earth, and the fifth also
—a laughable gap in my design—
and the sixth heaves aside

           damp ground
and purple shadow,

         and the seventh,
still underground, feels the sun's heat,
and deep

      in the stunned bulb, quick

               cells
divide and redivide,

        accelerating.

BALL

Nose down, she
               courses the back yard, searching
for her ball
        until she sniffs it,
               hidden
in tall grass. She pivots on her nose
and vectors in on it,
        from base
to apex
        of a frantic triangle,
her brown tail's white tip spinning
               like
a rotor. She finds it, snatches it,
and lopes in a long arc back to me.
As much as finding it,
        she loves
to hold it in her soft mouth,
               wriggling
with the pleasure of being a retriever
retrieving.
        Pure essence, bred to it.

When I think of beauty,
               I think of this
dog stretching to
        full stride, long
loose muscles undulating underneath
brown fur,
        until she's running
               too fast,
misjudges, smacks her ball
               into the neighbors'

magnificent azaleas, and scrabbles through them,
too focused on the zigzag ball
to ponder
            dignity, the sublime,
or love, and thus attaining them—
the body fully body till it drops,
exhausted.
            Tongue lolling on brown grass,
she stares at me,
            alight
with the exacting genius of her joy.

THESE PRIVILEGES DOTH THE WOLF HOLD TO THIS HOUR

The wolf is neither faithful nor unfaithful.
The wolf eyes everything—a sultan who
dines leisurely and then surveys his harem.
From lost antiquity he holds the right
never to be our symbol, no matter how desperately
we need a symbol, no matter how easily
he could shoulder the meaning that crushes us.
He is not a pack mule or a tractor.
He's a tongue, a claw, a tooth, a pelt, and though
he may become a hibiscus, he will never wear
the clothing of a hibiscus. The wolf eats jam
without bread, sucks wine straight from the grapevine, consumes
a dozen eggs at a mouthful—yolk, albumen, shell,
the pasteboard carton that they came in, nest,
white hen and strutting rooster, farmer and farmer's wife,
the traveling salesman and any jokes the latter three inspire.
He lives in the death of everything his red teeth puncture,
and so deeply does he breathe the fragrance of the lily
that he inhales loose petals, and when he sneezes
they stick like shipping labels to the cheeks
of all who stand before him. Marrow bones!
Marrow bones! Cracked and sucked until they whistle!
The wolf is neither faithful nor unfaithful.
The wolf eyes everything. He's merely choosing.

HAIL

Begonias and impatiens:
>   snapped. The hostas:
shredded.
>   Oak leaves crumpled on flat grass.
Caladiums: stripped to red stalks,
>   two limp
pink pennants dangling from crimped stems, and three
birds hammered from the sky
>   or from a limb.
Who knows?
>   But hammered dead
in my front yard. Two blue jays and
>   a sparrow.
Breathe,
>   I tell myself.
>   Death
>   is its own season, out
of sequence, lapping, overlapping
>   —crack!—
and the cold white stones seep into pounded grass.

GOAT GOD

At twilight, pale twilight,
a queer tune from deep shadow—
even in the city
a piping from green tangles
of box and honeysuckle,
an eerie lilt: our eyes brim
with easy, pleasing tears.
A song of love and mourning
at twilight: the mind
drifts and we dreamily
search upward for the moon,
then quickly walk away,
heads down, pursued
by cold, capricious laughter.
But the god of whims is quick
to fix his gaze and quick
to follow it. A flurry
of hoofbeats along
the edge of shadow. A glimpse
in tittering oak leaves
of the monster's dreamy smile,
the god's angelic
dissipated face,
and we desert the road,
forsake the fresh-turned furrow,
leave the car door open,
engine running,
and we enter, mesmerized,
the green kingdom, the green
enveloping dream he dreams
for us. In there, he falls,
like rain, on everything.

The goat god throws himself
on sheep and shepherd, goat
and goatherd, me and you.
Isn't this why we entered
his green realm, his dream? Aren't
his luminous demonic gifts
what we had gambled for—the sacred
deliberation of the wheel,
the meditations of the dice?
Strange babies, hairy and sly,
are dropping from our wives
and daughters. Strange lambs, their eyes
alight with god-fire, unfold
from our indifferent sheep.
And in the pasture, above
the wedding couch, by the cradle,
at the gray deathbed, we hear
from greenery the goat
god laughing with us
when we laugh, laughing at us
when we cannot laugh
sweetly, without bitterness.

PLANT TWO SEEDS

Plant two seeds, pluck the weaker seedling.

When wild seed litters the furrows and when
green worms swarm the cornsilk,
listen to the wren and finch.

Listen to the swallow when
                        mosquitoes
rise from the stagnant lake and cloud the sunset.
Listen to the brown bat and purple martin.

Listen to the bee when rose blossoms
bloom
gold at the center.

Plant two seeds, pluck the weaker seedling,

and listen to the crow when soft
                        corpses
bloat on the battlefield, on Fountain Square,
    beside the empty highway,
beneath the ornamental cherry.
Listen to the crow, the street dog, beetle.

Spartans died only for Sparta.

Plant two seeds. Death is never wasted.

KEYS

Freed
     from my winter coat, giddy
               with sunlight
gauzy through greening limbs, I pitched my keys
into honeysuckled
        air, higher and higher
and higher—toss,
        snatch, toss—until
they snagged the powerline.
            Neck craned,
I glared at them,
       twelve feet
           above my face.
I cursed. I stomped around my suddenly
unyielding house.
       I rattled both doors
and pried at all
       five windows. I'd locked them
against the world. Now
          they were locked on me.
I threw an oak limb at the dangling keys,
missed, threw again,
        for twenty timed minutes—then
the stick
     struck perfectly. The keys
bucked from the line.
        My house was mine again!
But first I stepped clear of the powerline
and hurled bright keys
        into bright air and caught them
—once overhead and once behind my back—

before I slapped the steel
                            key in the lock,
kicked
        the oak door open, and sang
                                "I'm home,
I'm home" into the sun-invaded hall,
the front
            door breached, the windows at my mercy.

HAMMER AND SCOURGE

Look in my eyes, vile rodents, and befoul
your quivering haunches, for I am black Slick, Hammer
of the rabbit, Scourge and Terror of the chipmunk.
O, Simon down the street has slain a few,
and Maxie over the back hedge has slaughtered some,
but Slick has yowled above a thousand corpses
while Maxie licked dried food off garbage cans
and Simon, simple Simon, licked himself.
Across the green yard I have scattered jay
and robin down, like blue and red confetti,
and even moles in their underground councils
speak my name, if they dare, late at night
with trembling voices and panic in their bowels.

When I address the weak gods, I screech "In!"
and they open the door, and open it again
when I screech "Out!" They offer me soft meat
and I, according to my whim, may eat it—
and that in my good time and at my leisure,
for I am black Slick, and grieving finches shriek
and wail for all the nestlings I have devoured
and will devour. I gobble them like gumdrops,
then lick their purple breast-down from my paws
while they flitter through the treetops, cursing Slick,
Death to the field mouse, Destroyer of the gray squirrel.

WHEN THE WEAK LAMB DIES

When the weak lamb
                   dies, the shepherd skins
the body, stretches
the skinned fleece like a little lamb suit
over an abandoned lamb,
                   the lamb's
front legs
           jammed through the front leg holes
and the back legs jammed through the back
                         leg holes—
the live lamb wrapped in the loved scent
of the dead one, and
                  the deceived ewe lets
the orphan suckle.
               Within a day,
when he begins to shit her milk
and she smells his shit and smells herself,
he's hers.
          This is what the dead
are for: for use, hard
               use, the duped
ewe giving suck and the orphan lamb
sucking more
             than he can swallow, milk
pouring down his chin, chest, legs,
soaking
         the straw and packed dirt,
                     flooding
back into his closed eyes, splashing the ewe—
a blessing so huge it looks like waste
as we choke,
            gag, gulp, gag,
                   gorge ourselves.

TOOLS: AN ODE

The cheap
        screwdriver reams the cheap
                screwhead,
and the dull blade burns white oak and splinters cherry.
The loose wrench
        torques the bolt on crookedly
and strips the thread. But guided by good tools,
the screw bites freely to its full length,
              the board
rips cleanly,
        and the hex nut weds its bolt.
Thin shavings rise in long unbroken curls,
each lovely in itself.
        The good tool
            smoothes
rough lumber underneath the unforced hand,
unwarps
       the warped board, trues
            the untrue edge
before it chops the mortise, cuts the tenon,
and taps them home
       in happy marriage. With good tools
the edge falls
      plumb and all
           four corners square.
The house holds snug against the crashing wind,
and there
     is order in the polity
and pleasure in the handmade marriage bed.

THE BOTTLE TREE

Shards of pink Depression glass swayed,
                        swung,
and twirled
            beside blue, green, and amber bottles,
pie tins, broken mirrors, and
                  whatever else
made sense to this believer who had killed
and resurrected
            his live oak—a tree
of glittering, a hoodoo shrine. At noon
the glass,
        from certain angles, blazed—
                    and blinded us
when we drove down the street. At night it flared
in headlights like the Resurrection,
                dazzling,
dangerous.
        And for this fireless burning,
he'd stripped the leaves.
They would have blocked the sunlight, hid the snakes,
birds, squirrels, mice
           he'd hung along the limbs.
They stank,
        drew flies. At night boys rumbled past
and blasted buckshot into the shining tree.
But to everyone who'd listen, I insisted,
"Maybe we could save it.
              Start over. He
could simply use the bottles. They're colorful.
They're clean."
        But this tree wasn't art, it was faith.

Once started, perhaps we too would string
                              dried flowers,
pop cans,
          and chicken bones from our bright tree.
And on the lowest limb we too
                    might tether
a crippled crow that screamed all night, and flailed,
fighting the lamp cord twisted to its leg.
It fought, fell, dangled
                         upside down and—screaming,
flailing—
          it air-clawed back to its bloody perch.
And as our tree grew stranger,
                         we'd believe
it grew more otherworldly, beautiful
and potent.
          When they chopped it down, we'd know
they feared it—and we'd love it even more.

We tried to understand what he believed
so we could mourn
                    almost appropriately
what we had made him sacrifice.
                         We failed.
We were the Romans. Our little town was Rome.
And Rome,
          where is it now?
                         Around the stump,
green twigs
          burst from unpoisoned roots and rose
in a loose circle, like uncertain acolytes,
tentative,
          but green, as I have said,
and multiplying. From the sidewalk, strolling by,
we all eyed them
               —believer, unbeliever—

and though we knew what they were,
                              we didn't know
what they
          might come to mean. And we eyed the stump
which stood amid them like, hauntingly,
                              an altar.
But to
        what god, what faith, what
                                heart's desire?
For there are many types of altar—and glory
beyond the confines of our longing.

WHY STOP?

Why stop? The dancers are
                                    still dancing,
though we now wait for slower songs
so we can
                    cool off, catch
                                    our breath,
and talk a moment. But why stop?
We love
                    to clasp and be clasped,
                                                prop
each other as we sway and let
our palms slide
                                just a little loosely
across each other. Why stop?
                                            Because
the crackle in the bass amp now pops
and buzzes?
                            The drummer drags, speeds up?
It doesn't matter. Waiters
                                    slap
their wet
                    rags on the table, sighing
theatrically.
                        But still, why stop?—
although we've drunk two drinks too many,
bump
                heavily off each other's hips,
and sing a bit too loudly. My cheek
caresses her
                        damp neck, and hers
is pressed to my
                                    damp shoulder. Why stop?
To start again when we are stronger.

THE HANGING GARDENS

Gone: The Palace of Forty Columns. Gone:
The Garden of Heart's Ease, The Garden of Roses.
Gone: The Garden of the Shah. And even
The Garden of the Throne is nothing now
but rubble unreflected in brown rain
drying in the ruined reflecting pool. Gone,
the hanging gardens built for a homesick queen
who missed the meadows of her childhood mountains.

A child pondering my old Book of Wonders,
I daydreamed of gardens floating over the desert
in never-ending bloom—green steppingstones,
each lush with lilies and bromeliads.
I thought they were wizardry, not work,
in the dry land of tamarisk and camel thorn.
Amytis knows. And doesn't want to know.
The gardeners hide from her. The cypresses
are lovely, yes, and the waterlilies too—
lovely the date palms lining the waterways,
and the blooming water hyacinths—but I,
because I'd read my Book of Wonders, knew
their purpose was to shade the channeled water.

As Amytis at nightfall ascends her garden,
turning tier on tier in the cooling dusk
in the present tense of our imagining,
she doesn't touch the waterlilies. They'll part,
uncovering the lead-lined troughs—reeds, tar.
Through gaps in ivy and purple clematis,
she sees and doesn't see the slaves' palm prints
fired in rough brick. Beside the river, she'd watched

young slaves slap wet clay into bricks, then pile
dry brush on them. Before they lit the piles,
one slave—she'd seen him and she hadn't seen him—
strolled the haphazard rows, pressing his palms
into the soft brown river clay and twisting.
(I've seen him do this. Why can't Amytis?)

Down the false mountain, dammed, channeled, pumped
Euphrates water cascades like a mountain stream,
murmuring like a mountain stream, purling
and chuckling over artful, moss-draped stones,
but when she isn't careful Amytis hears
the *shaduf's* splash and creaking, laden rise.
If her mind drifts, she'll hear the steady clomp,
the muted huffing of the ox against its yoke,
the capstan's squeal, the slip and drag, the rasp
and slop of chain pumps forcing water up the mountain.
Freed, it plunges, rippling like a stream,
shaded with ferns, protected by blue cedars,
and, along the streambed, cultivated moss
is painted with spoiled milk and brushed like velvet.

All planned: each brown bloom plucked and carried off,
and every barren spot is soon adorned
with a new rarity: white myrtle, rosy
oleander with its almond scent,
narcissus, bonarets from Scythia—
a thoughtful gardener calculating her
bedazzlement.
                    Impatiently, she prowls
the rooftop garden of her upmost terrace,
watching the blurred red sun disintegrate
and slide below the crenellated walls
of her dry kingdom. The first stars separate
from the harsh sunlight overdazzling them,

and her eyes open and she begins to see
what she has come to see.

She ascends an artificial mountain, descends
an otherworldly garden. Each paradise
adores its wolf, its snake, its scorpion.
She savors possibility: assassins
beneath the roses, demons in the willow.
Now, anything can happen, although it never does,
and I, a torchbearer, arise from the tall grass,
ignite my torch and join the path. She follows.
The upward path is now the downward path,
and on the way down—backward, dark—black leaves,
wind-lashed in flaring torchlight, lunge at us,
beat at their twigs. And when the leaves rip free,
pelt toward us, tangle in her hair, she laughs
and lets them stay—laughs, and follows me.
But not me really, and not the torch,
but torchlight as it slides
across white blossoms, changing them to moons—
blue, luminous and unattainable:
torchlight and nothing. An ache for paradise,
says my new Book of Wonders, pages filled
with new research and fresh equivocation
spilling from the past and past-perfect tenses:
a pile of dubious rubble in the desert.
A name that may have been a mistranslation.
A garden that was built by another, later king
for a concubine. Or wasn't built at all.
Or that was, at best, a mound of mud
planted with short desert trees and brush.
And through the wavering possibilities
I see her and I do not see her walking
the rectilinear spiraling ziggurat
uphill at dusk, downhill in moonlight;

walking through her own absence; picking her way
discreetly through rubble in the desert; circling
a mound too closely planted for her to climb;
walking the rectilinear spiraling ziggurat,
uphill at dusk, downhill in the moonlight
of a word Herodotus misunderstood.
Or understood. I see her and I do not see her.

STUMP

The gray wood of the oak stump, dappled brown, stopped
the axhead, which would not be stopped
by what lay between it and the crosshatched oak: fine white
neck feathers, almost down, were sliced into the ax wound,
fluttering. I'd call it fluttering
if they'd been large enough to flutter. They weren't.
Swaying, if they were tall enough to sway,
and they weren't. Riffling, if there were more of them.
Flailing, if the wind were fierce, and it hadn't been.
But even with no word for it, white fluff, blood-glued into the slit,
tangled in the wind's breath daintily though I could feel no wind,
could only see a movement for which I owned no name
move across a stump for which I have acquired too many:
altar, eschara, shrine, tope, chancel table—
the holy place as abattoir,
a spot where the gods whose blood I shared
took life, rendered it sustenance, placed it before me,
and made me pause to bless it as if it weren't
inherently blessed, teaching me not gratitude
but the forms of gratitude, so when, with age, I came
to thanksgiving, blessing, praise, I'd know them for what they are
    and how
to perform their offices.
                    Mensa, predella, delubrum, the Lord's table—
so I profaned the stump. I stomped on it
and sang. I flapped my elbows, crowed.
I knelt and pressed my hot face on the stump,
then stood and cut my head off. I raced down the yard
in crazy circles, blood spurting from my neck,
and when I, flailing, dropped dead at my own feet, I stood,
ran back to my imaginary head, and kicked it
to the foot of an unstumped oak,

and the earth's breath, which I could not feel,
fluttered, swayed, riffled the dry leaves,
touching each tongue separately, beseeching it to speak,
while I, with vulgar words I would have spoken
if I had known them, praised its silence, and at my feet
my severed head laughed until I also laughed.
I picked it up, replaced it on my shoulders,
and merged once more our two diverging laughters.

ACKNOWLEDGMENTS

Grateful acknowledgment is made to the following journals, in which these poems were first published:

The Atlanta Review: "Poem" ("Blunt daffodil spikes"), "Supper"; *The Atlantic Monthly*: "Dragonfly"; *The Black Warrior Review*: "Ashes" ("Bill gripped the can in both hands"), "The Bottle Tree," "The Daffodils Erupt in Clumps," "Hammer and Scourge," "One Threw a Dirt Clod and It Ran"; *Boulevard*: "We Were Merely Talking"; *Critical Quarterly*: "Catching Breath," "Why Stop?"; *Five Points*: "Edge"; *The Georgia Review*: "These Privileges Doth the Wolf Hold to This Hour"; *The Hudson Review*: "Purple"; *Image*: "The Chinaberry"; *The Kenyon Review*: "Hail," "When the Weak Lamb Dies"; *The New England Review*: "Bodies of Water"; *The Paris Review*: "Goat God," "Heaven," "Rain"; *Poetry*: "Tools: An Ode," copyright © 1994 by the Modern Poetry Association; "Babylon in a Jar," "In Alesia," "Stump," copyright © 1997 by the Modern Poetry Association; *River Styx*: "The Hanging Gardens"; *The Sewanee Theological Review*: "After Muscling Through Sharp Greenery," "Elegy for the Bees," "Plunge," "Ball"; *Slate*: "Night Class"; *The Southern Humanities Review*: "In the Red Seats," "Signs of a Change in Weather"; *The Southern Review*: "Ashes" ("My left hand joggled Johnny's arm"); *The Western Humanities Review*: "Keys."

The epigraph quotation by Sándor Weöres is from "The Colonnade of Teeth," in *Collected Translations*, Edwin Morgan, trans., Carcanet Press, Ltd., 1996.

For residencies that made possible much of the writing of this book, I'd like to thank Yaddo, the MacDowell Colony, and the University of Alabama, where in the fall of 1996 I served as the Coal Royalty Professor of English. Thanks also to Daniel Anderson, John Drury,

Mark Jarman, Erin McGraw, and Alan Michael Parker for their comments on early versions of the manuscript. I'm especially grateful to Ellen Bryant Voigt, for her encouragement and trenchant, thoughtful criticism at a crucial moment, and to Peter Davison, whose criticism was, once again, pivotal.